Seven ingredients for healthy sermon listening

1. Expect God to speak

Adam couldn't really be doing with sermons. There were a number of things he liked about church, especially the friends he had made and the music (when the new music group were leading). But not the sermons.

He felt he had to put up with those because it would look a bit off if he walked out when the preacher started. They just seemed dull. Faced with the entertainment choice between *24* and *The Sermon*, it was a no-brainer: *24* won, any day.

Beth was really looking forward to the sermon. Last Sunday she had gone up to the preacher and said: 'I'm so looking forward to next Sunday – can't wait'. He looked pleased, if a bit surprised. But Beth wasn't being a creep; she really did look forward to the sermon, with a sense of eager anticipation. She wondered what God was going to say to her. She felt as if someone had told her to expect a telephone call from the US President: all week she was, as it were, waiting by the phone. So when the sermon started she was paying close and eager attention.

Beth was right. And Adam was a fool. We are to listen to sermons expectantly because Jesus gives the authority of God Himself to the preacher who teaches the Bible accurately and prayerfully. Jesus governs His church by the written word of Scripture (which has been called His sceptre). The main way He does this is not by the written word being read, but by the written word being preached and taught. Of course, it is good when people who can read, do read and study the Bible; but it is vital that all people, without exception, hear the Bible preached.

IT'S A **VERY** SPECIAL DELIVERY

When Peter tells Christians they have been born again 'through the living and enduring word of God', he explains that: 'this is the word that was **preached** to you' (1 Peter 1 v 23-25).

Paul thanked God that when the first Christians in Thessalonica heard the good news of Jesus (Acts 17 v 1-4), they 'accepted it not as the word of men, but as it actually is, the word of God' (1 Thessalonians 2 v 13). Of course, the words they heard were spoken by human preachers; but they recognised that these words were at the same time the actual words of God. And it is not just apostles like Paul who can speak like this; Peter says that: 'If anyone speaks' (and the context is Bible teaching in church), 'he should do it as one speaking the very words of God' (1 Peter 4 v 11).

A word of warning, however: it is not always true that when we hear the voice of a preacher, we hear the voice of God. The preacher's authority is a borrowed authority; it's not because they are gifted or eloquent that preachers have authority, nor because they may be ordained, or have titles, degrees or qualifications, or are recognised by churches or denominations.

However, when the Bible is faithfully opened up, we are to listen to the preacher's voice as the voice of God Himself. The preacher stands in the great tradition of prophets and apostles who spoke the word of God. Unlike them, the Christian preacher cannot offer new or fresh ideas to add to the Bible. But like them, there is a borrowed authority to speak what God wants spoken. We ought to listen to this kind of sermon with the utmost seriousness.

There should be nothing casual about our listening, as if this were 'just another sermon' or simply 'what always happens at this point in our meetings'. When Ezra the preacher opened the written word to read and preach it, all the people stood up as a mark of respect and attentiveness (Nehemiah 8 v 5). In the same way, there ought to be a reverent hush as the Bible is read and preached in our meetings. Sometimes in sermons we will smile at ourselves and our foolishness (preachers do well from time to time to invite us to laugh at such things) but we will never be light or flippant about the voice of God.

Remember, we will not instinctively hear preaching as the voice of God. Our natural reaction is to take it simply as the voice of people. One of the wonderful things the Spirit of God does is to open our ears so that we receive it not just as the voice of people, but as the voice of God. We need to pray for Him to do this in us.

PRACTICAL STEPS TO TAKE

1. Look up next Sunday's Bible passage and read it at home during the week.

2. Pray for next Sunday's preacher in the middle of the week.

3. Pray often for yourself, that, by His Spirit, God will grow in you a heartfelt expectation that God Himself will speak to you as His word is preached.

4. If you can, try not to come to the sermon exhausted, but to come rested and ready to pay close attention.

5. Deliberately quieten your mind and heart before the sermon and say to yourself: 'This is when God speaks to me'. Pray again: 'Lord, speak to me. I am listening'.

2. Admit God knows better than you

Chloe hated Sunday's sermon. She was popular at school; everybody liked her. She thought of herself as a Christian, but wanted badly to keep in with all the different groups at school, whatever their beliefs. The sermon had been pretty straight about what Jesus says about the cost of discipleship and the need to be open about your faith before people. Chloe could see that if she really did that, some of her 'friends' wouldn't be quite so friendly. As she went home, her thoughts turned to whether the Bible was really quite as simple as the preacher had said. Surely there were other ways of reading the Bible that made it easier to fit in with everybody at school. Weren't there?

Dylan felt deeply challenged by the Bible passage preached on Sunday. He'd always been happy enough with his well-paid job and comfortable lifestyle. And being a Christian just seemed to add an extra layer of comfort, respectability and peace of mind on top. Now, as he listened to the challenge of Jesus to His disciples, he was unsettled. Could Jesus want him to change, perhaps change his giving radically, perhaps even change his job? Yes, the Bible passage really did seem to mean that. Dylan went home humbled and thoughtful.

Chloe and Dylan both understood the sermons. But their responses were very different. Chloe's response was to try to find a way around it; Dylan's was to bow before the teaching of God. You and I must not only take seriously the voice of God; we must bow the knee in submission when He speaks. We must come humbly to the preaching of God's word.

But we don't want to do that. We come to the Bible with all kinds of prejudices. We don't come to the sermon as blank sheets, like a new page in a notebook. On the contrary, we come to the sermon with our lives already scribbled over. We come believing certain things to be reasonable, and others to be incredible. We come accepting that some kinds of behaviour are normal and acceptable, whereas others are not. For the most part, we don't get these prior beliefs and assumptions from the Bible; we get them from our culture, from the places where our culture tells us what is normal, believable and acceptable. For example, from soap operas (someone has called soaps the sermons of our society), Or from our favourite blog, radio station, Facebook friendship group or magazine. And we get these beliefs from our own histories – from our parents, friends and experiences. So, what we really want is for the Bible to tell us we're ok, what we've done is ok, and what we believe is ok.

THIS COULD BE REALLY PAINFUL

But it isn't ok. It's not at all ok. Far from coming to the Bible as a clean sheet, I come to the Bible as a thoroughly messed-up person, unable to think straight, speak right or act as I ought. That means I must expect the Bible to call me to repentance and not to reassure me that I'm ok. It will never make me comfortable or complacent in my sin.

When Timothy had to lead the church (or churches) in Ephesus, Paul warned him that people 'will not put up with sound (ie: health-giving) doctrine. Instead, to suit their own desires, they will gather around them a great number of teachers to say what their itching ears want to hear' (2 Timothy 4 v 3). Comfortable doctrine makes me feel good about myself; it doesn't hurt. But health-giving doctrine does hurt.

This is one reason why faithful Bible teaching isn't more common in churches, because faithful Bible teaching will always cause offence. Sermons about the right way to do liturgy, or about church government, or about current affairs, or about the terrible sins of other people, or about the fascination of religions and philosophies will not upset me.

But the voice of God spoken by a faithful Bible teacher will get under my skin. It will cut to the core of my being (Hebrews 4 v 12, 13). It will challenge me to 'get rid of all moral filth and the evil that is so prevalent and humbly accept the word planted' in me (James 1 v 21). And I mustn't expect to like it. Sometimes I may even feel insulted. While Jesus was preaching against the Pharisees, a religious teacher (presumably not a Pharisee) interrupted Him to say: 'Teacher, when you say these things, you insult us also' (Luke 11 v 45). He listened to Jesus' sermon; he understood it perfectly; and he didn't like it at all. 'I don't like biblical preaching; I find it offensive,' you might think. Quite so; it is.

It's been said that it's very hard to get a person to understand and accept something when their salary depends on their not understanding and accepting it. In the same way, it is very hard to get me to understand and accept the teaching of the Bible when my comfort, my lifestyle, my complacency, and my selfishness all depend on my not understanding and accepting it.

To listen humbly is to be realistic about this. What is more, it is to recognise that there is more than one way to evade the challenge of the Bible. The simple way is just to say: 'The Bible is wrong, I don't agree with it, and that's all there is to say'. But the more common way in Christian circles (where we hesitate to be quite so blunt and honest in our rejection of the voice of God) is to find a clever way to reinterpret the Bible so that I can persuade myself that, although I must admit it looks as if it challenges me, in fact it doesn't. This preserves my impression of piety while safeguarding my rebellion against God. Beware the voice that says: 'Yes, I know Christian people of past centuries have consistently taken this passage at its face value, but now we know better and can see that it doesn't fit quite comfortably with political correctness or with western materialism (or whatever)'. To listen humbly is to admit that the Bible is right and I am wrong, that God is God and I need to change.

On our own we will never bow humbly before the voice of God. By nature we always rebel. We need to pray for the gracious work of the Spirit of God to humble our proud hearts.

PRACTICAL STEPS TO TAKE

1. Which parts of this week's preached Bible passage challenge your beliefs or lifestyle?

2. Does the passage clearly teach these things?

3. Pray for the work of God's Spirit to enable you to submit to what the Bible clearly says, and to help you to change.

3. Check the preacher says what the passage says

For **Finley,** the sermon is something that just washes over him, a kind of merging of his stream-of-consciousness with the preacher's stream-of-consciousness. If it's engaging, he enjoys the stories, the humour and the personality of the preacher. But he finds it a bit awkward when someone who hasn't been there asks him afterwards what the preacher said. Or, if the preacher is very clear, he may be able to tell you what the preacher said. But he'll be a bit stuck if you ask him what the Bible passage was, and how the sermon related to the passage.

Ellie is a great thinker. She reads the passage before Sunday comes, and then, as the passage is being read in church, already she is beginning to wonder what the preacher is going to say. As the preacher speaks, she is mentally trying to sort out how the preacher gets the sermon from the passage. She's the kind of (sometimes rather tiresome) person who will go up to the preacher afterwards and actually ask them where in the passage their second point came from. Preachers aren't used to that!

Finley is lazy; Ellie is wise. Listening ought to be an activity rather than a 'passivity'. Unless we want to be brainwashed, we ought never to hear or watch anything without engaging our critical faculties. If that's true for TV or a movie, how much more for sermons where the preacher claims the authority of God. We need to check that the preacher is actually using the only available authority, which is a borrowed authority that

only comes from teaching what the Bible passage teaches. So, we need to listen carefully to the passage and ask whether what the preacher says is what the passage says.

I was speaking to a friend called Mark about his church, where the preachers would say all sorts of fanciful things. They would start with the Bible, but before long they were flying around all over the place. Mark had only recently grasped the need to listen actively. I asked him: 'How is church going?' He replied: 'You've ruined it for me! Previously, I just accepted what the preachers said. But now I keep looking at my Bible as they talk and ask myself: "Where did he get that from?"' It's a good question: *where did he get that from?* If preachers can show they got it from the Bible, then I must humbly submit to the authority of the word of God. But if not, then it's just the opinion of one human being against another.

Some people find it helpful to have paper and pen and take notes. This focuses them on what precisely the preacher is saying and helps them to see whether or not it comes from the passage. Others find note-taking a distraction and prefer to devote their energies to listening. Whatever strategy you use, always have in mind the question: *where did the preacher get that from?* We are not asking how well or badly the preacher preached, in terms of communication skills. We are asking whether the message of the sermon was unpacking and pressing home to us the message of the passage.

It's worth saying that it's not only academic people who can listen actively like this. Some people have experience of reading and studying books, and some of those skills may come in handy with the Bible. But anyone can understand enough of the Bible, when it is clearly read and taught in a language they understand, to be able to see at least roughly whether the preacher is building the sermon from the passage, or just using the passage as a springboard for saying what they wanted to say anyway.

It is the work of God, by His Spirit, to open our minds so that we listen clearly, think clearly, and discern clearly whether a sermon is true to the Bible. By nature we cannot think straight. So again we need to pray for His work in us.

PRACTICAL STEPS TO TAKE

1. Read the passage or listen carefully when it is read.

2. What do you think is the main point of the passage? This may be signalled by repetition of something important, or by being in the punchline (for example, of a parable), or by being the theme that runs through the passage. Is the main thrust of the sermon the same as the main point of the passage?

3. Are there any surprises in the passage, ie: things the Bible says that we wouldn't expect it to say, or that it says in ways we wouldn't expect it to say them?

4. Who was the passage originally written or spoken to? Are we in the same situation as them? In particular, if they were before Christ, we need to be careful what parallels we draw; we can't simply apply it straight to ourselves. After all, it wasn't written to us. It was written for us (for our benefit) but not directly to us.

5. Why do you think the Bible writer wrote this passage? What is the passage intended to achieve in its hearers?

6. Pray as Martin Luther used to pray: 'Lord, teach me, teach me, teach me'.

4. Hear the sermon in church

Hamsa is an avid sermon-listener. She has hundreds of downloads on her iPod from famous preachers all over the world. She listens to them on the bus, on the train, while washing up, while going to sleep. She has clocked up hundreds of hours of solo listening. She's not in church very often these days, because she can get sermons that are so much better from the internet.

Gareth isn't always so keen to hear the sermon. Sometimes his attention wanders. But he's generally there, week by week, in his home church, listening to his own pastoral leaders. 'OK,' he thinks, 'they're not as eloquent as the preaching super-stars, but they're the ones who know me'. He has a feeling they pray for him. When he shakes their hand, they have a real interest in him. He'd rather listen to them preach him the word of God.

Gareth has got hold of something fundamental, and widely neglected, about preaching. The normal place for preaching is the gathering of the local church. We are to hear sermons as a people gathered together; they are not preached so that we can listen to them solo later. The word 'church' means an 'assembly' of men and women who gather physically together. There is no such thing as 'virtual church'. The assembly of the people of Israel in the Sinai desert was called (literally) 'the church in the wilderness' (Acts 7 v 38).

This church was defined by the call of the word of God to gather under the word of God. It began when God said to Moses: 'Assemble the people before me to hear my words' (Deuteronomy 4 v 10). This set the standard shape and pattern for the people of God, who are gathered by the word of God (God takes the initiative to summon them, and us) and gathered to sit together under the word of God ('to hear my words'), to be shaped together by His word. God's purpose is not to shape a collection of individuals to be each like Christ, but to form a Christlike people.

We may even say that preaching is properly done only when the people of God in a local church gather. When we listen to an MP3

recording of a sermon,
we are not listening
to preaching, but to an
echo of preaching that
happened in the past.
Listening on my own to
a recording can never
be more than a poor
second-best to actually
being there with the
people of God in a local
church. It is better to listen to the
pastor you know, and who knows you,
than to hear a recording of the well-known preacher you
don't know, and who doesn't know you.

When we listen to a sermon together, we are accountable to one another
for our response. Hearing while gathered is significantly better than
hearing alone. When I read my Bible on my own, it is all too easy for my
thoughts to drift, my eye to stray from the page, my heart to be inattentive
to the word. If I sit and listen to a recording of a sermon, it is all too easy
to hit the 'Stop' button, either actually or metaphorically, as my attention
'switches off'.

When I gather with my brothers and sisters to hear the word preached,
it is still possible to hit the 'Off' button. I can look out of the window; I
can read the 39 Articles at the end of the Prayer Book (if it's that kind
of church), or read Wesley's instructions for congregational singing in
Christian Hymns (if it's that kind of church); I can doodle; I can day-
dream. But it is not quite so easy. For my brothers and sisters around me
might notice, and that would be embarrassing! Besides, they might even
talk to me afterwards about the sermon, and I'd hate to have to admit
that I have no idea what it was about.

What's more, when we listen together, you know what message I've
heard, and I know what message you've heard. I've heard it. You know
I've heard it. I know that you know I've heard it! And you expect me to
respond to the message, just as I hope you will. And so we encourage

one another and stir up one another to do what the Bible says. By being with you, I make it easier for myself to respond the way I know I ought to respond. I can listen to a very challenging Bible passage preached on a recording, and if I ignore it no one knows. But if I pay no attention to the sermon I heard with you sitting beside me, you will know; and I would hate you to know I wasn't listening!

When we listen together, we respond together. The Bible is mostly addressed to the people of God together. This is disguised in modern English translations, where we cannot tell whether 'you' is singular or plural. It is more often plural than singular. The Bible's purpose is to make and shape the people of God, which means in practice the local church. So the first question to ask ourselves is not: 'What is God saying to *me*?' but rather: 'What is God saying to *us*?'

It is worth giving a bit of thought to how we talk about the sermon in conversation after the meeting. It is all too easy either to snipe at the sermon's weaknesses, its lack of structure perhaps, or its dullness ('I really struggled to stay awake in that'). Or just to say how much we enjoyed a particular story, anecdote or joke ('I loved the story about...'). Instead, why not make an effort to say something about how you hope to respond to the Bible truths in the sermon? ('I was really challenged to ... Were you?' or 'I was really encouraged by ... How about you?' or 'It was so helpful to be reminded of ... Don't you think?') Or perhaps there is still something in the Bible passage that really puzzles you; how about asking someone: 'Can you help me understand what ... means?'

We ought to make it a priority to be there to hear the word of God, and to encourage others to come with us so that we can hear the word together. Again, we cannot do this on our own. By nature, we won't want to hear the word of God corporately, because it's much too uncomfortable. Besides, we might lose face in front of others, having to confess our sin and learning to repent, believe, love God and love them. So we must pray for a deep love for our fellow-Christians and a Spirit-given desire to sit together under His word.

Practical steps to take: These have been combined with the suggestions in the next section.

5. Be there week by week

Indira has had some terrific sermon experiences. There've been times when the sermon has really scratched where she was itching, times when she can testify that God has spoken to her so clearly and strongly. She can tell some great stories of times when her life was changed for the better by Bible preaching. But she's only in church about one week in three. Sometimes she is away for the weekend. Sometimes she just stays at home. After all, she reasons, so often when she goes to church the sermon just reminds her of something she knows already.

Jake is there for the sermon week by week. If you go to his church and he's not there, it usually means he's sick. He's not been a Christian as long as Indira. He doesn't know his Bible as well. But he's growing a lot faster as a Christian. He knows he has a short memory and needs a lot of reminding. It doesn't trouble him to hear what he's heard before. He develops the habit of just being there week by week and letting the Bible message soak in again and again.

Jake will become more Christlike year by year. Indira is likely to be a spiritual firework, full of fizz-bangs for a short time, but with no lasting light.

We shall see (number 7) that there is a 'today' urgency about listening to sermons. We need to listen today, repent today, and believe today. But that doesn't mean that every sermon will scratch precisely where we are itching. Preachers love it when we say to them: 'Thank you. That was just exactly what I needed today'. But most sermons won't be even approximately what we think we need today. In fact, most Bible passages will not seem at all relevant just now.

But that doesn't mean we don't need to hear them. Every good doctor knows that a patient may come with presenting symptoms that mask a deeper illness. If she just treated the bits where patients feel pain, many patients would die. God knows what we need much better than we do.

And it's a misunderstanding to think that by some divine magic the Bible passage I happen to be reading today will be precisely what I need today, and then again tomorrow, and the next day. That would be a remarkable series of coincidences. But the Bible was never intended to work like that. We say: 'I want to hear God speaking to me today'. Well, He will speak, if I hear the Bible faithfully preached. But He might not teach me what I **think** I need to hear today.

The Bible is not designed to give me a series of instant fixes. It is God's instrument to shape and mould my mind and my character into the likeness of Christ. And that takes time. I need to listen to the Bible passage being preached today, and to turn my heart to God in submission and trust today, not only because I may need that passage today, but because I may need that passage tomorrow. And tomorrow may be too late to learn it. I need to start learning it today, so that it can begin to sink in and change me. And this takes repetition, and reminder. Peter understands this when he writes: 'I will always remind you of these things, even though you know them' (2 Peter 1 v 12).

So we need, not a random series of sermon fixes, but to sit together regularly, week by week, under the systematically preached word of God. And as we are taken through the teaching of the Bible by patient exposition, gradually Christlikeness is worked in our characters, our affections, our desires, our decisions and our lives. We need to pray for this supernatural, gradual but lasting work to begin and continue in us, as we hear the word of God preached week by week.

PRACTICAL STEPS TO TAKE

1. Keep count for six months or a year of how many weeks you are in your own local church to hear the sermon. Make a note of the different reasons why you're not there.

2. If you find you're away more than you realised, and more than you ought to be, take some practical diary action to make sure you're there more regularly. Come back from holiday on a Saturday. Get back from a visit to friends in time for the Sunday evening meeting. And so on.

3. Be aware of the others in your local church as you listen to the sermon.

Talk to them afterwards, not only about how we should respond as individuals, but about how the Bible passage should shape the church.

4. Pray often for the work of God's Spirit to shape both you as an individual and your church as a body of Christians together.

6. Do what the Bible says

Keith, by and large, is pretty happy the way he is. He finds Christianity interesting. He feels welcomed and generally affirmed in church. He even enjoys a good preacher's 'beat-up' about sin. It makes him feel good to lament how awful the world is, and how terrible other people's behaviour is out there. He very much wants the person sitting next to him to obey the Bible, as well as the people he reads about in the news. But it doesn't occur to him most weeks that he himself needs to be changed by the grace of God.

Lakshmi is deeply aware that she needs to change. Every week she is convicted of some way in which she is not like Jesus. It may be the cutting word that slipped out, or the jealous thought she harboured, or the selfish money she spent. But whatever it is, she comes to the sermon knowing she can't risk staying the same. So when she understands straightforward Bible teaching, she longs to put it into practice. She prays week by week for a heart that responds to God's word with loving, practical obedience.

'Do not merely listen to the word, and so deceive yourselves. Do what it says' (James 1 v 22). The purpose of sermons is to change us into Christlike people. We are to be those who: 'with a noble and good heart … hear the word, retain it, and by persevering produce a crop' (Luke 8 v 15), where the 'crop' refers to the fruitfulness of a Christlike character. When Paul encourages Timothy to persevere with preaching (2 Timothy 4 v 1-5), he reminds him that the purpose and profit of Scripture is 'for teaching' (what we ought to believe), for 'rebuking' (what we ought not to believe), for 'correcting' (how we ought not to behave) and for 'training in righteousness' (how we ought to behave). Preaching has

a comprehensive brief for belief and behaviour (2 Timothy 3 v 16).

We mustn't expect sermons to entertain us. We live in a culture of entertainment; we can generally find amusement at the press of a remote control button. One reason people have stopped coming to listen to sermons is that, if they come for entertainment, they can find better entertainment elsewhere. It is rare for a sermon to be able to rival the special effects of a Batman or a Bond, or the brilliant script-writing of *The West Wing*. Most preachers are bound to fail, and mistaken to try.

Nevertheless, from time to time people will come to some preachers to be entertained. Herod enjoyed listening to John the Baptist preach, even though John condemned Herod's wrong marriage. Paradoxically, Herod managed to screen out conviction of sin and just enjoy the style and manner of John's speaking (Mark 6 v 14-29).

There was a time when the people loved coming to hear Ezekiel preach; somehow it was as entertaining as listening to a popular love-song: 'Indeed, to them you are nothing more than one who sings love songs with a beautiful voice and plays an instrument well, for they hear your words but do not put them into practice' (Ezekiel 33 v 32).

We see this today in the Christian sub-cultures of celebrity preachers. There are a few preachers whose style and manner is so good that we can listen to them for hours. Tastes differ, as for music, and some will say 'we are of X'; others, 'we are of Y' (insert your favourites) (see 1

Corinthians 3 v 4). We might shop around churches until we find a style of preaching to suit our taste, because our aim is to be entertained, rather than to be taught, rebuked, corrected and trained in righteousness.

However, it is a great mistake to think we have it in us to obey. On our own we *cannot* obey. We are slaves to sin, unable to help ourselves. We cannot even repent without God working repentance in us (eg: 2 Timothy 2 v 25). It is God who opens our hearts to respond to His message, and not just at the start of the Christian life (Acts 16 v 14). We need to pray for God to open our hearts week by week to His truth.

PRACTICAL STEPS TO TAKE

1. After this week's sermon, write down all the ways you wish that other people would obey that teaching. Don't hold back. When you've written it all down, tear it up.

2. Now let's get to business. Write down as definitely and precisely as you can some action you need to take to obey this Bible passage. It may be a change of attitude, or an alteration in the way you speak, or some action you need to stop doing, or start doing. Whatever it is, write it down.

3. In a week's time, and then a month's time, look at what you've written and ask yourself whether that Bible passage made any difference to you.

4. Pray, pray and pray again for God to work obedience in you to His word.

7. Do what the Bible says today – and rejoice!

Mike loves preaching. He really believes this is how God speaks to him. He is on the edge of his seat as the sermon starts, notebook in hand. He has a great file of sermon notes and is developing awesome skills of checking whether the sermon is biblical. He is convinced the Bible is 100% trustworthy. But his wife hasn't actually noticed much change in his lifestyle over the 10 years he's called himself a Christian. He knows a lot. But doesn't seem to change a lot. And somehow even the note-taking feels like a worthy chore.

Nell isn't so good at analysing Bible passages. To be honest, she feels a bit out of her depth when her friends discuss it at house group. She is very aware that there's so much she doesn't understand, and she carries around with her all sorts of unanswered puzzles. But when she does grasp something, her conscience won't let her get away with just filing it in her sermon notes. She wants to know what she ought to do about it. And then she does it. She actually changes her lifestyle. She has an uncomfortable habit of actually doing something about the Bible teaching she hears (uncomfortable, that is, for her friends like Mike). But, paradoxically, Nell finds herself rejoicing in the whole experience of responding to the sermon and walking before God with a clear conscience.

If we were holding elections for the church council, we would do well to vote for Nell rather than for Mike. Every sermon is urgent. When Moses preached his last recorded sermon, he said to the people of Israel: 'See, I set before you *today* life and prosperity, death and destruction' (Deuteronomy 30 v 15). The psalmist says the same: '*Today*, if you hear his voice, do not harden your hearts' (Psalm 95 v 7, 8). The letter to the Hebrews takes this verse from Psalm 95 as its text for a strong word about urgency in Hebrews 3 v 7 – 4 v 13. The keynote is 'today'.

Every time the Bible is preached, we ought to repent again and trust in Christ again. The Bible doesn't just call non-Christians to repent and believe. It calls Christians to repent and believe; and it does so today. As long as it is called 'today' (which, of course, it always is!), we need to be challenged not to be hardened by the deceitfulness of sin (Hebrews 3 v 13). When we become Christians, we do not leave repentance and faith behind; on the contrary, we enter a life which consists of daily repentance and faith. The turning of our hearts towards God and His way is never a thing of yesterday. The decision we may have made yesterday is proved genuine by the fact that we do the same turning of the heart today.

Every time we hear the word of God preached, we must respond today by a turning of the heart away from sin (repentance) and towards God and Jesus Christ (faith). It is not that we become Christians again day by day; that is not necessary. As James puts it, the word of God has already been implanted and has taken root in our hearts; and yet we still need to receive it humbly and urgently day by day (James 1 v 21).

This is true whatever part of the Bible is being preached. No part of the Bible is there simply to inform us, or for our interest only; always it calls us to turn to God, perhaps in a changed belief, or a refreshed delight, or a new behaviour, or an altered value-system. But the turning must be done today. The story is told of the devil training his junior devils. He asks them what they are going to tell human beings. One is going to try: 'There is no God'. The senior devil thinks it's worth a try, but doesn't think many will be foolish enough to fall for that. A second suggests: 'There is no judgment'. The senior devil thinks that's better, but still doubts he'll have much success, because people have an inbuilt sense of accountability, an understanding that our actions have consequences. 'Any other ideas?' 'How about, "There's no hurry"?' pipes up a third. The senior devil warmly congratulates him: 'That is exactly the message that will be most widely believed and will do the most harm'.

Every time we listen to a sermon, the devil will whisper in our ear: 'That was good stuff. Why not do something about it tomorrow?' And we instinctively want to agree, because tomorrow never comes. As the Red Queen says to Alice in *Through the Looking Glass*: 'Jam tomorrow, jam yesterday, but never jam today'. The devil echoes this and says: 'Respond to the preaching tomorrow, respond to the preaching yesterday, but never respond today'. And if we listen to him, we will never respond. As Augustine prayed when his sexual sin was challenged: 'Give me chastity, but not yet'.

NO RUSH! YOU HAVE PLENTY OF TIME!

To hear a sermon and not respond is worse than not hearing it at all; it makes us more guilty than we were before. As Jesus said about the unbelieving Jews: 'If I had not come and spoken to them, they would not be guilty of sin' (ie: not as guilty). 'Now, however, they have no excuse for their sin' (John 15 v 22). As Charles Simeon puts it, every sermon 'increases either our salvation or condemnation'.

So when the devil whispers: 'Why not respond tomorrow?', we must reply: 'No, today as I have heard His voice, I will not harden my heart'. This daily urgency of response will gradually, over the years, shape our character.

But yet again, we cannot do this unless God works in us. Moses understood this perfectly when he appealed so urgently in Deuteronomy 30 for a response 'today'. In verse 6 he holds before them the promise that: 'The LORD your God will circumcise your hearts and the hearts of your descendants, so that you may love him with all your heart and with all your soul, and live'. If we are to obey today, we must cry to God to work in us again today.

Like Nell, when we develop the habit of hearing and obeying, we will find a paradoxical joy in the whole experience. Yes, it will be challenging and often uncomfortable. But it is a wonderful and joyful thing to understand, repent, and walk before God with a clear conscience. We may find that listening to sermons becomes a matter of deep joy (of a kind that our non-Christian friends may find very surprising!). It is a wonderful thing that the living God, who made the universe, speaks to us today and calls us to walk in delightful fellowship with Him.

PRACTICAL STEPS TO TAKE

1. Ask yourself how the preached passage shows you an attitude, or words, or actions that need to change.

2. Then change, urgently, praying for grace to enable you to repent.

3. Ask yourself in what way the passage encourages you to trust in God and in Christ afresh. Then resolve, urgently, to put that fresh trust into your life as God helps you.

4. Enjoy preaching, not as entertainment but as God's regular gracious invitation to walk with Him, rejoicing in a clear conscience.

Preaching that makes a church Christlike under grace takes a double miracle: the sinful preacher must be shaped by grace to preach; and sinful listeners must be awakened by grace to listen together week by week in humble expectancy. Only God can do this. So praying before the sermon is not a formality. Unless God works, the whole thing will be a waste of time. But God loves to change us through preaching, and He loves it when we pray to be given fresh repentance, renewed faith, joyful obedience and a corporate Christlikeness in the local church. So let us pray for this with confidence.

How to listen to bad sermons

Some will have turned straight to this section. 'The trouble with all that ideal stuff in the first section is that you just don't live in the real world. You don't have to put up with the sermons we have to endure in our local church. Have you anything to say to those of us who are subjected to bad sermons?'

There are three sorts of bad sermon, and how to listen well depends on which sort we are talking about. A sermon may be dull, it may be biblically inadequate, or it may be heretical. We shall take each in turn.

How to listen to a dull sermon

We don't know what sort of teaching style Paul had in Troas, but we know he spoke for a long time and that one young man went to sleep and fell out of the window (Acts 20 v 7-12). Maybe Paul was dull, or maybe Eutychus was just very tired to start with. These things happen.

By 'dull' I mean a sermon that leaves a lot to be desired in its style or presentation. It may be chaotic, unstructured, and hard to follow. It may be dense, trying to cram in much too much for most of us to absorb in one sermon. It may be delivered in long, complex sentences that sound as though they are read out of a commentary poorly translated from German. It may dot around the Bible in a bewildering manner. It may lack any lightness of touch, so that listening is like eating a very heavy pudding with nothing to cut through the stodge, or like walking in a dark room with no windows to bring light into the building. There may be little or no help given in working out the implications of the passage for our lives. In all sorts of ways, the sermon may be poorly presented.

> It may dot around the Bible in a bewildering manner. It may lack any lightness of touch, so that listening is like eating a very heavy pudding

Let us suppose, however, that this dull sermon is biblically faithful and accurate, and delivered by a preacher who believes the truth, has

prepared as best he knows how, and that the sermon is surrounded both by his prayers and yours. If this is so, we ought to do all we can to listen with the aim of profiting by it. We may be able to encourage the preacher to get help with presentational skills. Certainly we should pray for our preachers, and encourage them whenever they shows signs of improvement (a text or e-mail of thanks for the good bits is so much more effective than a stream of complaints; if the preacher has to tweak the junk filter to remove your messages, you have achieved little!).

But above all, we must search our own hearts and come to the sermon praying for God's help to listen as attentively as our bodies will let us (caffeine may help). My advice is not to worry that quite a bit of the sermon may go over our heads or bypass our consciousness, but to ask God that some part of it may stick and be turned in us to repentance and faith. Try taking notes, or at least having paper and pen with you, with the aim of jotting down a verse or truth that can take home and respond to. Try going with a friend and agreeing together not to spend lunch lamenting the preacher's inadequacies, but rather, sharing positive Bible truths that you have learned or been reminded of, and praying together for God's help in putting them into practice.

Suppose now that the sermon is well-presented. It is interesting, easy to listen to, and clear. But the more you listen, the more you wonder if the preacher has a good grasp of the passage he is supposed to be expounding. You keep asking: 'Where did he get that from?' Somehow, the sermon seems to import all sorts of things not in the passage, or to screen out important things in the passage that do not feature in the preacher's understanding of Bible truth. The sermon seems to you to be wrong in places, and to lack the Bible's balance in others. How should we listen to sermons like this?

The first danger to avoid is developing a critical spirit. Some of those who listened to the Lord Jesus were 'waiting to catch him in something he might say' (Luke 11 v 54). Their hope when they went to the sermon was that they might find something wrong. With Jesus they never could; with our preachers, we generally can! After all, we teachers all make mistakes in what we say (James 3 v 2). But there is something wrong if fault-finding is our great aim. For then the sermon will just make us feel good about ourselves, how clever we are or how well we know our Bibles; but it will never move us to repentance and faith.

The second danger to avoid is being gullible and credulous, believing whatever any preacher says, so long as they say it plausibly and well. So we need to be always asking whether the sermon opens up the Bible. Like the inhabitants of Berea, we ought to search the Scriptures to see if what the preacher says is really true (Acts 17 v 11). But again, let's focus on the parts where the preacher has got it right. Rather than dwelling on the bits that might have been out of balance, let's pray for God to apply the bits that came from the passage to our hearts and lives.

> we ought to search the Scriptures to see if what the preacher says is really true

It may be possible and appropriate quietly and courteously to help a preacher gain a better grasp of Bible truth. Priscilla and Aquila did that with Apollos, and the long-term benefit to the church was considerable (Acts 18 v 27, 28). A wise preacher will always be glad to be gently challenged and questioned by honest enquirers. If correction is not possible or appropriate (perhaps because we are visitors, or much more junior than the preacher, or the preacher is unwilling to be corrected), then we can still pray to take away something that is true and put it into practice (in the same way as we would for a dull sermon).

How to listen to a heretical sermon

The short answer is: don't! But first we need to ask what the difference is between a heretical sermon and a biblically inadequate sermon. In New Testament terms, what is the difference, for example, between the teaching of Apollos, which Priscilla and Aquila corrected, and the false teachers of 2 John, who were not to be welcomed at all, let alone allowed into the pulpit (2 John v 10, 11)?

An old definition of heresy suggests it has three parts. First, it is an error in something central to Christian faith and not something peripheral. Someone is not a heretic if they get the millennium wrong (whatever you think 'wrong' to be), or if you think they are in error about church government, or the proper age or mode of baptism. They are a heretic if they deny that the man Jesus is the Messiah come in the flesh (2 John 7), or redefine sin so that behaviour which excludes people from the kingdom of God is treated as good (eg: 1 Corinthians 6 v 9, 10).

Second, a person is not a heretic if they get something wrong by mistake, and then put it right when they are corrected. They are heretics, however, if they hold obstinately to teaching which the Bible shows to be wrong. Most thoughtful Christians hold some opinions tentatively. We are not sure, and we know we're not sure; we wonder. And in appropriate contexts we may share our tentative ideas with others, even if some of them may be wrong. This is not heresy.

> a person is not a heretic if they get something wrong by mistake, and then put it right when they are corrected

27

Third, it is only heresy when the person actively seeks to teach this error in the church. A private opinion is not heresy. The mistake of a Christian is not heresy. The Bible reserves its sharpest scorn for false teachers in the New Testament, and for false prophets in the Old Testament. People who privately believe something that is in error may endanger their own destiny, but they are not heretics. A heretic is not only a false-believer but also a false-*teacher*.

So we are considering here a church where the preaching goes against some central Christian truth, does so dogmatically and persistently, and does so energetically, seeking to persuade others. The way to listen to these sorts of sermons is to stop listening to them! That is to say, we ought to move away from that kind of church and find a church where they believe and teach the Bible faithfully. We will not look for an exciting church, where the preaching entertains; we will look for a faithful, Bible-teaching church.

How to get better sermons

The hearers contribute to the sermon almost as much as the preachers. We who listen to sermons have a vital part to play. In 2 Timothy 4 v 3, 4 there is a revealing insight into the place that the congregation have in making preaching profitable or (in this case) unprofitable. Paul warns Timothy that the normal state of affairs in 'the last days' (2 Timothy 3 v 1)—that is, the whole period between Jesus' first coming and His return—will be for people not to put up with healthy (sound) doctrine, but to make sure they get preachers who will tell them what they want to hear. If they want to be affirmed in their sin or greed or materialism or sexual misconduct, they will encourage, welcome, train and pay preachers who will tell them that these things are all right. It is very hard to be a faithful preacher in a congregation like that!

> when they listen stony-faced and give no word of encouragement, it is very hard for even the most faithful preacher to persevere

Not all poor preaching is entirely the fault of the preacher; the congregation has a vital part to play. When a congregation makes it clear that they are reluctant to hear faithful preaching, that they want the sermons to be shorter and play a more marginal part in the meeting, when they listen stony-faced and give no word of encouragement, it is very hard for even the most faithful preacher to persevere (although they ought to, as Jeremiah had to). By contrast, a congregation eager for faithful, challenging Bible preaching is much more likely to get it.

7 suggestions for encouraging good preaching

1. **Pray for the preachers.** Pray specifically that they will work hard at the Bible passages (1 Timothy 5 v 17) and preach them faithfully, passionately and in a way that engages with us.

2. From time to time, **tell the preachers you are praying for them** and looking forward with expectancy to the sermon. That will be a great encouragement and incentive to them to prepare well.

3. **Be there.** You may be surprised what an encouragement it is just to have you there, and what a discouragement to have you absent.

4. **Thank them** afterwards for things you learned. Don't flatter or just give them very vague comments about how good it was (if it was). Try to be specific and focus on the biblical content of the sermon rather than just stories, anecdotes or illustrations. Tell them if there was something in particular that you found helpful.

5. Be prepared to be **constructively and supportively critical.** Ask the preachers to help you see where they got a particular point from the passage; this will sharpen them up if, in fact, it didn't come from the passage, or indeed the Bible. It will encourage them to stick to the Bible more next time. Be humble and respectful in the way you do this; remember, it is much harder to preach than it is to criticise preaching.

6. **Relate to your preachers** as one human being to other human beings. Remember that the best sermon by a remote preaching hero, heard on an MP3 recording, is no substitute for the word of God preached by a human being face to face with other human beings in the context of trust and love.

7. Be on the lookout for **gifts of preaching** and teaching in the church, and be ready to tap someone on the shoulder and suggest they develop these gifts and get further training. Mention these ideas to the pastoral leadership team in your church.